NO ORDINARY WORLD

NO ORDINARY WORLD

poems by
Mekeel McBride

Carnegie-Mellon University Press
Pittsburgh & London 1979

Acknowledgments

The Agni Review: "The Juggler Defines His Art," "The Knife-Thrower's Wife," "The Gravity of It, The Ground Rules," "Asking for Help at a Late Hour," "What Light There Is," "The Source of Light," "Meditations Before and During Sleep," "We Bring This Weather With Us"; *Alembic:* "Tumbled Lullaby"; *Antioch Review:* "Holiday"; *Blue Buildings:* "A Change in Weather"; *Chowder Review:* "What Cannot Be Tasted," "This October," "No Child of Earthly Kitchens"; *Ironwood:* "The Mathematician's Vision"; *Kayak:* "The Keeper of the Sea," "The Need to Talk," "Ahead, Too, There Is Dancing," "No Ordinary World," "Real Life Unlike the Cinema"; *The Little Magazine:* "Why We Write Poems"; *The Nation:* "The Whale Poem"; *Pequod:* "Black Boy's Death by Drowning"; *Poetry Northwest:* "Learning to Untie the Knots"; *Racoon:* "The Origin of Snow."

I wish to thank the MacDowell Colony, the Radcliffe Institute, and the National Endowment for the Arts for their generous support.

For My Family

With special thanks to David Gordon Campbell, Bob and Dolores Russell, Mailee Scott, Stephen Dobyns, Charles Simic, Jane Shore, Jim Dalsimer, George Starbuck, and Joel Noe.

Some of these poems first appeared in a limited edition volume, *A Change in Weather,* Chowder Chapbooks, 1979.

The publicaton of this book is supported by grants from the National Endowment for the Arts in Washington, D.C., a Federal agency, and from the Pennsylvania Council on the Arts.

Library of Congress Catalog Card Number 79-51606
ISBN 0-915604-29-9
ISBN 0-915604-30-2 pbk.

Table of Contents

"And you smell the smell of oak leaves now,"
he said, "now the air is cold. They smell
to me more alive than people. The trees
hold their bodies hard and still, but they
watch and listen with their leaves. And I
think they say to me: Is that you
passing there, Morgan Lewis? All right,
you pass quickly, we shan't do anything
to you. You are like a holly-bush."

St. Mawr
—D. H. Lawrence

I

The Whale Poem

I am a swimming forest;
each rib in me
a harp
no wind will hurt
into music.

Make your claim, Eve,
make it.
For garden I depend
not on your god,
not on the hand

of lightning, harsh
scripture of the harpoon.
This planet is blue.
I do not ask
to be forgiven.

The Keeper of the Sea

What is fame anyway but the one person
who dares to wear white to the funeral,
that daily funeral funneled into milk bottles,
hidden in the lip of a coffee cup?

I am acquainted with myself and a few others
who carry black umbrellas, custom-made rain clouds.
In spite of storms, the grave prophecies of crows
I keep dreaming of Marlon Brando.

Now he is half-Indian, hunting for me
in the heart of the Dakota badlands.
Now he is the keeper of the sea
sunning me under the soft wave of his blue hands.

Always, he wears white suede and there is
about him the faint smell of horses and the tropics.
I do not give out his name
at cocktail parties. I make sure

everything else is in order:
my black umbrella, my balanced checkbook,
my ordinary sorrows. So it is going
to rain for another hundred years.

So everyone I love is going
to die. Even I will thin down to a crown
of weeds in an empty field. Still, that does not
stop Mr. Brando from gathering me in his arms

as if I, by carrying the dream of him in my head
have made an edible bread, honey-filled pastry
from the black pillows of those who lie surprised
by nothing on their endless beds of stone.

What Cannot Be Tasted

The would-be suicide comes into my kitchen
wearing a black bowler hat.
He opens his umbrella;
nails fall all over the floor.
"These are my teeth," he says,
"and I am dying of hunger.
Neither your blue spoons
nor your Chinese spices can save me."
And indeed, he is as thin
as the neck of a violin.

I give the signal and my parakeet
begins to sing Vivaldi.
I ask my children the onions
for their clean white coats.
Anything will do in an emergency:
green peppers, French newspapers,
the pearl from a widow's necklace,
white mushrooms.
I stir the stew with a stiff rose.
Steam rises like bread for Houdini's ghost.

The would-be suicide has taken off his hat.
In flour that has spilled on the table
he traces the outline
of a sleeping cat. He smiles
at knives bitten sharp by stars,
wooden spoons remembering
the tough thrust of sun up their spines,
while the slight suspicion
of something not be tasted
teases him to eat.

The Juggler Defines His Art

It matters little to him. He can take stones
in his hand or birds or bits of burning wood
and storm the sky as sure as a meteor shower.

Ask him how and he will sigh, saying
"Ah, I have married Lady Gravity
and these, these are my children."

Then ask him what it is
he loves so much that he is able to suspend
all belief in the solid world.

And he will say, "The heart is an orange,
a porcelain cup, a closet
that has not been opened in years.

My own heart I am no longer sure of.
Once it was a golden watch.
I gave it to the woman I loved;

each jewel in that watch, a planet.
Each planet, a place where we were safe.
Now I am no longer sure of anything but

time passing on her lost wrist
as I pass hand over hand, far above
your amazed faces, my bright and weightless life."

The Gravity of It, The Ground Rules

We stand by a river, late.
Two people who once
were lovers. Trees surround us like extras
on an opera stage.
Their branches hold no leaves, no
relief. You lean
to me and I long for life without gravity,
without ground rules.
You say, "For a moment, now, nothing is
unfinished," then leap
lightly to your bicycle, wheel
away into the dark
like some departing constellation.
It takes patience
to make my body move in this stiff landscape.
Stars escape me or the meaning
of stars. And I think, such a havoc
heaven holds over me
in the name of order, or mythology.

The Knife-Thrower's Wife

The knife-thrower's wife stands
stranded in danger's glittery geography.
A paper heart is pinned in sequin
to her breast. She would be afraid
if she could see her husband caress
each knife, mouth her name before aiming.

But the spot-light sews her eyes shut.
"Slut," he says to himself, "you whore."
Now she hears them coming, a sound
like bees, a sound of bullets. She
wonders if there is a war somewhere.
Applause. A held-breath pause.

He places his blindfold carefully. He aims
as close to her heart as he can. And then
it is over. She steps forward, sees
her silhouette set out by ice-pick,
sword, all manner of sharp things. She
joins hands with her husband. They bow.

She sees he loves his knives more than
he loves life: his, hers, it doesn't matter.
This is what makes her take her place
again and again, glad for the knives
that need her, that wait to surround her
like a crowd of adoring suitors.

Odysseus and the Sirens

A blue muscle from the moon
pulls our ship toward a sheaf of rock
where they lie. They are as naked
as scissors and sing with the same
promise of release. Their red songs
rise around us like flamingos.

One sings the hardship of making soup
from bark, diamonds, desert clouds.
She sings we can fill her heart,
her hungry belly if we abandon the memory
of timid women waiting elsewhere.
She says she will die unless we feed her.

Another sings of waking to doors
freshly painted white, windows
opening onto almond trees;
how our hearts will be made clean again
after she has claimed us.
She is wrapped in a winding sheet.

And so they sing one thing and mean another.
I cry, in spite of myself,
to be untied, to be able to follow
their songs that glitter
like strings of diamonds on the dark sea.
I am the only one who can hear.

The others have stuffed their ears
with wax, dust. They wander dumb,
uncomprehending through an air that is awesome
with promise. The knots in the rope
I asked for tighten at my chest
as the ship tips, turns slowly away.

This October

for Annie Farrow

One branch loses its leaves
like the sleeve of a silk kimono
slipping from a dancer's arm.

What gold there is cannot be used
for money. Even the apples
ask to carry more weight,

prove gravity again and again
with as much grace as possible. Wind-fall,
fruit ripe as a sorcerer's moon, who

is living in my house? She
sees clearly now only herself
in the mirror. Dressed

in the expensive silk of solitude
she dances without magic. Such
relief, this rich music

that makes itself heard from even
the most common object: glass box
of mending thread, three sun-

skinned peaches, clean sheets
on the bed beneath the window.
Now at dawn she wakes once

before the time when she will stay awake,
listens to the few strange birds
that will remain within her hearing

through the most pointed seasonal warnings,
through winter's worst weather. They
sing in spite of fallen

leaves, impending snow, all
that's been lost; they sing, they
sing in spite of everything.

The Need to Talk

The poem you asked me to write
places me at this plain table,
at a time when my neighbors lie blessed in pairs;
the evidence, Biblical,
their ark, sleep which eludes me.

Hardest to bear is the light from my lamp, late now,
in December. I live
alone, would like to believe
this light is more than the loosely woven cloth
of insomnia;

would like to believe my life
is more than
what surrounds me. My shoes
surround me, paired up like couples
at a private funeral
each with their own reasons for walking away.

For a moment I hold
my ground, gaze at the box of paper before me
as blank as calendar pages for next year.
Here, the funeral goes unattended;
love's body lies cold,
embossed by the kiss of a literary rose.

Nothing has died that I cannot do without
but even as I write this, I set my head
down on the table,
for a moment, for a moment only,
and wish there were
someone here to talk to.

Tumbled Lullaby

And what is the sound of the sea?
I can't remember. No gypsy celebration
here. No bells.
No beginning that I haven't seen before.

For instance, falling asleep
is not so different
from falling in love; I hear wind
inside the pillow

sweep its sad hands through a field
of dry corn stalk. Such desolate clatter.
Scarecrow mutters a lullaby that tumbles away
as if in love with the wind.

He believes it goes unnoticed. No,
this has nothing to do with love. Here,
rain's the only likely weather. Some infant
god, raging for no reason,

throws down, hard, his pretty money,
his priceless legacy. For me
this weather means nothing more
than a cold walk home,

a hard night trying to identify
in which corner now
the dust of loss collects,
waiting to take over.

Asking for Help at a Late Hour

Clotho was one of the three Fates.
It was her business to spin
the thread of life.

Asking for help at a late hour
I hear the man on the phone
long distance ask,

Is there something
from this side, something
I can do?

I look out the window.
There ought to be a face
framed by dark astors

or even the moon,
mimicking as it floats low,
rescue.

There is nothing but his
voice, a colorless thread
stolen from Clotho's sewing box.

It surrounds me, dark garment,
good disguise
in this equally dark room.

Somewhere now our voices meet.
Maybe over Iowa,
that middle-ground of hard winter,

unexpected harvest.
Our words cross and in crossing
caress like the hand

that is careful as it sweeps back
a wing of hair
that has fallen across the sleeper's face.

What Light There Is

Now the distance between us is a field.
What light there is I gather and plant.

Above me clouds build themselves into storm,
into dark animals that splinter the sky with desire.

Where are you in this field? Beyond it,
taking apart the calendar box by white box.

Where am I? Here, walking in the dark,
waiting to see what will break earth first.

Now the air is thinner than it once was.
What wind there is touches me

the way an old man touches with surprise
the memory of himself as a child

and it is this wind, a little thinner
from travel, that days later will touch you.

Ahead, Too, There Is Dancing

To prepare myself for this I break the mirror
then piece it together on the soles of my shoes.

From a length of black silk I cut my coat.
The needle is the tooth of an extinct animal;
the thread, thinned from a convict's flag.

When my shadow whines like a leashed dog
I recognize the place as mine.

When my feet grow as heavy as sleep,
when the bones in my spine clack together—
bad-luck dice, I know.

Here, on this road where the ash of Pompeii
still darkens the sky and trees burn
like books with the evil of the world

I find a poem in the shape of an antelope.
It leans beside a golden river
drinking the shadow of a wing, a cloud.

Here, too, I meet my own death.
Like an old woman it continues alone,

eating roots, glad for the spider
that nests in her house of clay and dried grass.

And I am safe although the bones of the dead
shine like hooks through the transparent earth,

although the dog that follows at my heels
carries a human heart in its mouth.

And when I grow lonely from the long walk
I listen to my feet as their dancing

echoes against the stone drum of what lies before me
and returns with the news
that ahead, too, there is dancing.

II

Monologue of the Woman Carrying Ten Trees

Too many to put down.
I need them
for what they might be later.

Birds bury their most cherished stories
in the catch-all of my cautious ear. Dogs
fall in step with this queer walking forest.

Winter will seem warmer
after it filters through my ten green
children. Looking through ice-latticed windows

at a world gone
sugary and soft, I could cut
logs, I may carve bowls

or build a house within my house
as shelter to the secrets
a stranger leaves me. Too many

to put down. Sometimes I cannot move unless
I say their names and let
that rhythm reach my feet:

first is Ginko gold with grief,
second Aspen, no relief. Then Cherry,
Maple, Elm and Oak: you will always live alone.

Now one step and then another, next
step, next step then another.
I keep them for what they might be later.

The Mathematician's Vision

Nine, filled with an air of importance
floats from my hand, leaves me who will never
get even one step ahead of myself.

Eight fences the weary country of nothing.
I live in one world, my love in another.
The wind weeps around our separate houses.

Seven is the gallows tree.
Love's thin body sways back and forth
teaching me to dance on air.

Six sleeps dreamless, that old woman
who lives in a house with every window broken.
Look, her belly is fat with the food of death.

Five is a snow man the blind child made.
When it melted, I found blue pebbles
in a wooden box, the body of a robin.

Four shines, a silver cup.
I use it to catch rain. The reflection
of a drowned child smiles from the surface.

Three forms a pair of wings in a dark sky.
I am never sure of the body:
something I wanted, going away.

Two is the swan on a black lake.
A moon hangs in the willow there
like a mask forgotten after carnival.

One, the staff cut from dark oak.
I lean deeper and deeper into my life
on this third leg, this seeming logic.

Black Boy's Death by Drowning

Walter Bridges
1958-1972

I wonder why I always do things wrong.
Davis and Earl kept on top
of the lake like rubber ducks.
I dived, watched them disappear.
They survived. Their legs
dangled from a bright sky
like bicycle handle bars, far away.

I reached for air, caught only a rough rope
of water. Sky came back black as my hand
and a minute later I knew
something on the bottom wanted me.
Not the way rats used to hiss, nibbling
my sleep like I was their
gingerbread boy, brown enough and sweet.

I thought again of Earl, our
jelly sandwiches wax-paper wrapped,
my tennis shoes hidden on shore.
I tried to shout. My lungs filled
with water as easily as if it were air.
Afterwards, I drifted to these weeds.
They wrapped me mummy-tight, murmuring apologies.

I never had a mother.
The weight of her presses me
as flat as freshly ironed sheets.
Dusky streets chalked for hop-scotch
tighten at my neck. I'm made of lead,
late for school, can't run.

There's something scared inside
wants out, can't shout anymore.
I am the one who got away
thin as the reeds that surround me.
Whoever I was, Walter Bridges,
now rises empty and aching
in the swollen sun.

Holiday

Last night I dreamed of dying.
It was a holiday.

I dreamed the death room was pink
with two single beds.

The sheets were sealed to the bed
with wax.

I knew there was a dog on the other side
of the door. I'd seen him as I entered.

He was black,
eyes blank as winter windows.

When I knocked to be let out, he howled like wind
scraping the inside of an abandoned house.

Somewhere in the room with me
was my grandmother's body. I couldn't find her.

When I closed my eyes
I saw summer filling the curtains
like the breath of a small child singing.

No Child of Earthly Kitchens

I owned no raincoat and in the season of storms
was sent to school under my mother's umbrella.

It was the color of pale sherry. The ivory handle
kept about it the faint smell of perfumed wrists.

It never carried me away although I wished it
often enough that I can still see beneath me

people with their umbrellas like black morning glories
growing small on a polished street.

And I see, too, my house as tidy as the shoebox
for a hurt bird; the flat horizon

filling out as purple and plump as an eggplant.
And when the dark arc of the umbrella sets me down

and when my feet again touch stubborn ground
I am no longer a child of earthly kitchens

but find the geometry of clouds closeted in my heart
and in my hair, the strange blue perfume of storm.

Learning to Untie the Knots

"We walk on earth and have no need
of wings." And suddenly he heard
his father's loud voice saying:
"I had wings. I had wings."
—Aldous Huxley

Neanderthal dark.
My father walks the rooms of his house
well past three every morning
like a burglar baffled at plate
someone had promised was silver.

His footfall on hard wood
wakes me now. I want him to tell me
why he can't sleep, what keeps him
walking these dark and childless rooms
but all he does is repeat,
"Don't know, don't know . . . "

His hand is tender as it closes
the door to the room where his wife
is sleeping. It is too late to wake her.
It is too late. He moves
to the living room

motions toward his painting
of shore-shattered spray,
furious oceans, then points
to the opposite wall
where two

candle-thrown shadows wait.
We stand alone. Somewhere beyond
blank glass, the sea
turns over, his wife turns over.

An enormous heave of dark dreams
touches him, shrinks the rope of another knot
until it cannot be untied.
Our shapes are hour-glass dust.
We drift apart.

I would ask him where he goes,
tomorrow's weather, what time tells
from the luminous dial, just to make him
speak but black numbers spin a nimbus
at his back and it is late.

Ahead of me he has found his way
into the dark by following
torn curtains, table tops, chairs,
feeling how everything he touches now
might have been more.

Part of a Family History

In the room where my grandmother
used to sit, the window
still admits light
as if that light were the arrival
of a friend, arms folded
around a cloud of Queen Anne's Lace.
Even now it seems she is there
in a green print summer dress
waiting for me, the dark stones
on her fingers
shining between us like secrets.
But she is not there and when she left
she took my name for her last word
saying it quietly and I did not come
saying it once again
and the dark door opened.

Stopping Places

for Nancy Esposito

This September's sun glazes everything
until the season seems pure renaissance. Suddenly,
nothing will go wrong.

You restore two illuminated manuscripts,
one called *Evening Later;* the other,
Walking in the World.

You own no house but in your one small room
you realize this time you will survive
with more than simple minimum.

Now you say the word *plum*, pleased with its round vowels.
Now you say the word *apple*. In your pocket, a list
of birds that can survive the winter.

Still, a grasshopper fiddles its taut warning
that this mardis gras of clean sky,
copper-colored leaves, love allowed

cannot last. Its stricken singing says,
"Snow soon. All trees as thin as stick and bone.
Stone on the heart,

stone." And it does begin
to snow, so deep there is no trace
of where you have been walking in the world.

On your table, the book of *Evening Later*
lies open. What marks your place is a yellow leaf
pressed between two transparent wings of wax.

Fat, sensuous apples sleep deep in the dark cellar.
Often and even in the coldest weather
you unglove one hand

to touch in your coat pocket
a chestnut that you rescued from November.
It is as polished as a small holiday.

As you hold it in your hand you can hear
a thin aunt speaking of how to spice
the Christmas goose.

The fireplace whispers, "warm socks,"
warns snow to stay beyond the window pane.
Your uncle lights a fat cigar.

Smoke rises in thick blue ribbons. Gifts
are wrapped in red and gold. Placed together
they glitter like an oriental palace.

You are the child charmed by an unmarried cousin
who holds her glass of wine to fire-light.
Goblet, flame, her opal ring

all speak secrets concerning the dark spectrum
of desire; there are things she cannot tell.
And everywhere, everywhere, the smell of apples!

We Have All Come Home Again

What a poor doll house our childhood must have been
that we bowed to the big mirrors,
the enormous beds that barely hold us now.

We come back, still dressed in blue scarves,
red boots. At the sound of our voices, the dog
that has been dead for years rises gladly.

Our parents are in a far part of the house.
They are stooped slightly like trees
bearing the weight of a wet, unexpected snow.

They bend to us, with weightless arms
they welcome us into the life we will have
to live without them.

The Source of Light

Romaine Smith Russell
1884-1974

1.
She wakes as if struggling
out from under a heavy net.
This time she knows me.
"If you loved me you would take me
home." It is evening. My shadow
fills the room: grey, motionless snow.
Soon she sees her husband
who has been dead two years
standing beside me. She begins to cry.

2.
Before she died, she said,
"Red candles. Take them away, take them."
Later, "I can hear birds now. It is raining?"
The dead, in their coats of rain,
began marking out another
small kingdom in the dark.

3.
Over the phone the nurse's voice sounded
like a bird trying to fly through glass,
"She's dead. You can come for her now."
When I got there I saw that the dead woman
still reached for me as if I could hold her
to earth; she was as weightless
as the thin body of the moon.
Even the trees reached for her,
felt only the passing of light.
Then it started to rain.

4.
After her death she weighed
no more than the thought of how it would feel
to have wings. I know
because I carried her home.
Arranged around my neck, her arms
were like the bones of a hummingbird.
She kept repeating,
"Same dream. Same old dream."

5.
I placed her on a quilt sewn sixty years before
and tried to mend a blouse.
The eye of the needle was burning.
Thread thinned to smoke in the opening.
There was the sound a moth wing makes
against a window and another sound
of something almost singing.
They slipped away;
the thread slipped away.

6.
Three days before the body
could be burned
I combed her thin hair, plaited it.
It was soft, already soft
like dust and smelled of the first rain
after years of drought.
I could feel nothing of myself,
only the soft wreath of her braided hair.

41

7.
She was dressed in blue for the burning,
a dress she'd never owned while alive
although I dreamed her wearing that dress
months before I knew she was ill.
In that dream she looked different,
as if standing inside a mirror.
I called to her but she was singing
and maybe didn't hear.

8.
When we knew her body was burning
we were not ready.
The fire started.
We were not ready.
Her blue dress floated around her
as if she were dancing
and the wind she danced in
would undo her death.
Fire unwrapped the sight of her sinking
into hospital sheets. Clearly
she was in the country
where once she had been young,
silhouetted for us then and years later
in any doorway,
as if someone had just passed through
leaving only a shadow
burning with light at every edge.

III

Meditations Before and During Sleep

for Ed Lefevour

Consider the waltz; consider bears
that dance in spite of chains, their fur
scarred by ticks and disobedience.

Consider your loneliness; the mailbox
empty except for a mockingbird's nest,
the mirror that promised you everything
and then went blank.

And think of roof-tops at dusk
as if they had been drawn by a child
who is wearing a light blue smock;

your hands as they sleep
remembering a weight of pearls,
bodies they have memorized,
departures they have signalled.

Consider the anagram of sleep
in which you have just created yourself.

Silence grows like a white camillia
from the mouth of the mime;
and the walls with their inner chambers
keep secret the shoes of your childhood.

Consider that somewhere, in a room
just beginning to grow dark,
a room in Cheyanne perhaps,
or Green River, Wyoming

someone folded among shadows
is saying, softly, your name.

Consider those shadows, the dusty window,
the geranium that strains and stretches there
its stiff and coppery leaves for news of the sea.

The Mapmaker's Recurring Dream

He returns every night, the man
who loved me once. And always
he is as perfect as an eclipse.
He walks the roads I chart by day.
An opal-colored lake by which he stands
was first discovered
among the rare inks on my desk.
He feeds on the faulty, frail clouds
that have no map for where they go.
Constellations, the clear
first quarter moon
are matted in his brown hair.
"I'm here," he says, in a voice
as slow as the ascent of a snowy egret.
"Do not be afraid. I've brought you
ancient China
silky with dragons and peonies.
I've brought you
a small town in Oregon
where the women wear plain dresses
and their men bring them
gifts of apples and feathers."
It's poverty I wake to
morning after morning
in the painful country
of the uncreased pillow,
the lonely mirror
and the fear I'll never fall
asleep again.

Why We Write Poems

"Ten thousand Chinese have come
to plant rice in New Hampshire."
—Stephen Dobyns

Rice will not grow in New Hampshire.
The Chinese do not know this.

They travel with small white flutes
and are not afraid of winter.

Their hats are silk,
five blue cranes embroidered on each one.

After the arrival, they sit in a field of snow,
share their rice with ravens.

Then they begin to play their flutes.
The music sounds like two sisters

singing of rain forests, the slow ascent
of thousands of cranes.

No Ordinary World

This is the story of one love rooted in sand,
as sensuous as an orange.
It feeds me with the honey of longing.
It is my third eye that opens only
to see the dreaming world more clearly,

the world in which you come toward me
as if from a great distance. You are untroubled
by gravity, rising slightly with each step
in a landscape heavy with stone.
Your body is the country an exile dreams of.

We are no longer in an ordinary world
of shared spoons, proper fences,
fish that speak sensibly of tides and the net.
When you kiss me you keep me
a little longer from responsible houses,

houses where I made the mistake
of staying too long and was in danger
of never dancing the tango again, nor could I
understand the amorous chatter of cats.
I was unable to draw speech out of voiceless things

there among the tame snakes, fountain pens
and children with cheeks of tapioca and common tears.
Look my love how all around us the walls of convention
shudder like a Babel tower. Only we two speak a true
language, stand on ground ungoverned by gravity.

We Bring This Weather With Us

The sea sets down its surprisingly
tame waves one after another
the way a reader regularly turns over
the pages of a book he can't abandon.
It's as if we brought this weather
with us and you have mapped the clouds,
put each one in its place.
They obey. Their medieval
architecture stays respectfully
in the background, will not
bother us with siege or sudden storm.
I devise this sky that seems
windless but still supports
a whole citizenry of kites:
dragon, serpent, butterfly,
tying a kind of Chinese heaven over us
for the entire afternoon.
We put the blanket down,
unpack the basket. And there!
the cheese with its golden tongue
tells folk tales from Amsterdam.
And strawberries the size
of small purses open to show
all of summer's money.
We talk or don't talk and if
there's tension or some unspoken sorrow
then it's in the taut wing-like sail
of a ship so far out to sea
it seems a toy that we
could push off to India
with one small breath.
But nothing's wrong.
There is enough sun for me

to wear my hat without pretension.
"Old Riviera style," you say.
Paper flowers from 1930
poise on the broad straw brim.
And your shirt is such
a perfect shade of blue that the sky
falls in love at first sight, spends
the rest of the day
following you.

Real Life Unlike the Cinema

for Jack Cunha

Undress me like no French cinema
clip

in which the lover whispers
because you are of earth . . .

while the camera momentarily
concerns itself with her lace dress

draped across a chair
and then it's morning,

nothing naked but
omission.

Make me
naked, take each button out of place,

a sun escaping
its thin night slit. I want

our bodies lightly starred
with salt, ascension;

the sheets on your unmade bed
ravenous around

us.
Kiss the tips

of my fingers until
each one burns.

It's tropical
apocalypse I want, sweet not

like honeycomb, not like table
sugar. Here

abandon the hunger
that keeps hunger whole.

Crush glass, crush bone;
the known world is no longer known.

From a Life-Time Long After This

Awake or half awake I wonder
why stars linger as they do, disguised
as salt that I taste on your skin

and hidden in your skin,
an arcane history of cinnamon
or sandlewood; spices of a kitchen after holiday.

In my one brief dream, you have asked for me
to stay. Outside your window, in a nearby tree,
the white cradle of a cloud anchors uneasily.

And the train that midnight engineers
through this strange place
might take us anywhere.

Oh, sleep love, sleep. I lie
awake. On the blackboard of insomnia
I'll chalk in a happy ending
for everything.

The Origin of Snow

Once again, snow tries its old disguise;
promises that the knife of loneliness
will lose its evil intention,
relent, open only imported oranges
where summer still hoards
the last taste of sultry weather.

Snow promises that the words
I meant to say
will be softened into sweet flour
from which I'll bake a healthy
bread all winter.
But I am not hungry

for anything the tongue
can test as false or true. Somewhere
someone I love is sleeping
in a room with no staircase.
And stars to him are nothing
more than stars and he knows only
that he needs another blanket;

does not know this obscured landscape
bears the weight of what once
was the moon; a moon that fell
for something love couldn't say
and, entering our atmosphere,
broke into unaccountably cold
stars that soon will settle everything.

Paradise Seen as a Practical
Aspect of Survival

You lie sleeping in a poem,
snow outside unable to become
again anything but
snow and you will sleep
like Beauty for as long as
ink lasts on this icy page.
I want you

to be warm. Here
is the word for blanket,
a quiet blue, a kind of
unobtrusive wool.

The world outside your window whitens.
The space between things deepens.
Listen, let me
say something tender to you.

There is at least one day
of good weather waiting for you
folded like the hum of magic
inside a harmonica.

And the Paradise River sleeps
as pliable and yielding as a question mark
inside your kitchen faucet
waiting for you to release it, allow it
to drop the miracle of desire,
its white diamonds
into the deep cup of your every-day waking.

Bird in the Hand

Bird in the hand, yes, but one that sings
as it sits there, even better. Singing things
like *June* or *firefly*, *foxfire* or *large harvest*; sings
that what you want is now yours or will be soon.

You wanted rain? Here's a cloud, a thin
rope of lightning to anchor it. All night, water
falls in soft Bach-like staccato.

You wanted something growing? Something
that would fill both hand and heart? Here's
canteloupe, sweet and ripe as the sleep you just left
and someone waking next to you to share it. Sooner

or later, Bird isn't there. No matter.
When you wake up, the trees still stand.
From those green cathedrals notched thickly with initials,

the fingerprints of angels, Bird goes about its business
making jewelry for the ear: emerald, onyx
or that one-note nameless pearl of hope. No matter,
no matter that you cannot hold it.

A Change in Weather

1.
I didn't want to introduce the moon
into all of this.
It was innocent and besides
it needs another coat of paint;
needs to clarify
its position on the politics of loss.

2.
I survived this time on snow.
And stars? A cold spice
that seemed comforting at the time.

3.
By February, the clouds have failed.
They lean on stop signs.
They are the ragged coats too large, too loose
on the firm shoulders of statues.
They multiply listlessly.

4.
Some days the sky is so gray
even the stage-hands can't find the curtain.
In a stunned tree I hang
three black lanterns: crow-
light.

5.
My plants refuse to play this bad-weather game.
They put out new leaves daily.
Like small town newspapers
they announce engagements, garden parties,
the sighting of a lightning bolt
in the Queen's otherwise clean closet.

6.
Those flowers that I left in your house.
They are not flowers.
They are the satin hats
of a literalist. They are
sick of winter, that's for sure.

7.
Daffodils shaped like antique telephones.
Familiar with Midas and his polished fingers.
I need to talk to you.

8.
Suddenly everything is out in the open.
But midnight never cleans its pockets.
Stars. Spare change. Occasionally
I talk to statues. Chiefly
I rely on other people's lighted windows.

9.
For every step I take
a pilgrim must take three
even though our destinations are the same.
Some pilgrims make the mistake of stopping.
We notice them as statues.

10.
Sky: a very blue arrow.
All around me,
evidence of battle:
crocus, iris, lilac
lift dangerously out of the earth
like Rilke's angels
or the oddly formed letters of a foreign alphabet.

11.
In another world much smaller than ours
each drop of rain is a fortune teller's globe.
That's what's falling all around us:
glass hearts, life histories
we refuse to claim as our own.

12.
A jay quits its usual jabber.
Its solvent coat assures
that the quality of color blue
has improved, almost
promises that there will be
a change in weather.
Spring. Its song is two-
syllable, sounds like a window
opening, sounds like a human
voice repeating, "Lightly, lightly."

Carnegie-Mellon Poetry

The Living and the Dead,
 Ann Hayes (1975)

In the Face of Descent,
 T. Alan Broughton (1975)

The Week the Dirigible Came,
 Jay Meek (1976)

Full of Lust and Good Usage,
 Stephen Dunn (1976)

*How I Escaped from the Labyrinth and
 Other Poems*
 Philip Dacey (1977)

The Lady from the Dark Green Hills,
 Jim Hall (1977)

For Luck: Poems 1962-1977,
 H. L. Van Brunt (1977)

By the Wreckmaster's Cottage,
 Paula Rankin (1977)

New & Selected Poems,
 James Bertolino (1978)

The Sun Fetcher,
 Michael Dennis Browne (1978)

A Circus of Needs,
 Stephen Dunn (1978)

The Crowd Inside,
 Elizabeth Libbey (1978)

Paying Back the Sea,
 Philip Dow (1979)

Swimmer in the Rain,
 Robert Wallace (1979)

Far From Home,
 T. Alan Broughton (1979)

The Room Where Summer Ends,
 Peter Cooley (1979)

No Ordinary World,
 Mekeel McBride (1979)